CAREERS IN
RETAILING

CAREERS IN
RETAILING

Loulou Brown

sixth edition

**KOGAN
PAGE**

The author would like to thank Alan Julyan of Speechly Bircham, solicitors, for help with the new employment law.

First published in 1982
Second edition 1986
Third edition 1988
Fourth edition 1993
Fifth edition 1995
Sixth edition 1997

Kogan Page Limited
120 Pentonville Road
London N1 9JN

British Library Cataloguing in Publication Data

A CIP record for this book is available from the British Library.

ISBN 0 7494 2390 0

Typeset by Northern Phototypesetting Co Ltd, Bolton
Printed and bound in Great Britain by
Clays Ltd, St Ives plc

Contents

Contents

Introduction

Is this the Job for You?

Questions you should ask yourself:

- ☐ Do you consider yourself a sociable person?
- ☐ Are you good at figures?
- ☐ Will you work at weekends?
- ☐ Are you quick on your feet?
- ☐ Have you got the gift of the gab?
- ☐ Do you like talking to people?
- ☐ Do you like doing lots of different jobs?
- ☐ Are you physically fit?
- ☐ Do you like working hard?
- ☐ Do you like hustle and bustle and being at the centre of things?

If you've answered yes to all these questions, you should think about a career in retailing.

This book is about shops and the jobs available for people who work in them, from sales to store management. It is hoped it will be a useful guide to anyone who wants to know more about retailing, and who might be thinking of making a career in the field.

Jobs available in retailing are set out in detail in Chapter 4 and illustrated with case studies. They are further illustrated by descriptions of a number of companies operating in different areas of the industry in Chapter 3. There are details of the products they sell, the company structure and the internal and external training schemes available. In most large, and some small, companies there are many opportunities for promotion and for varied and exciting careers.

In the sixth edition of *Careers in Retailing*, in addition to a radical structural change, there are a number of new sections. 'Is this the job for you?' in Chapter 1 and 'Top tips for getting into retailing' in Chapter 7 are aimed to help you focus on retailing, the skills required, the environment you will be working in and the personal characteristics of an individual best suited to working in the field. Chapter 8 looks at future trends in retailing and the areas where jobs are most likely to increase, while for the first time a 'Further reading' section lists publications to augment the information provided by this book.

Because companies have different rates of pay for similar jobs, it has been decided not to outline salary scales. Details of these can be obtained from individual organisations.

When this book was first published in 1982, the possibility of degrees in retailing had not been considered. During the past decade, however, the industry has been transformed and it is now innovative, dynamic and economically significant. It was Sir John Harvey-Jones, no less, who said that 'the retail sector is one of the great British successes where we can appropriately hold up our heads against the best world competition'. In the past few years, education and training have been intensified and there are now many degree courses to train managers to cope with the increasing scale, complexity and competitiveness of the industry. Details of universities and colleges offering degrees, their addresses and phone numbers are listed in Chapter 10.

Since 1994, new legislation has allowed all stores to open at any time of the day or night, apart from Sundays. This has meant that some stores have started to open for 24 hours several days a week. Legislation regarding Sunday trading has meant that all large stores, are allowed to open on that day for six hours. Because of the increased opening hours there has been a marked increase in the adoption of flexitime arrangements and part-time work.

It is very important before you start work to make sure what your contract of employment stipulates about how many hours you are being employed for each week. If possible, for your own convenience, you also need to know exactly what hours you are expected to work. So if you are thinking about a job in retailing, please look very carefully at the revised, expanded and very comprehensive section on employment law in Chapter 6, pages 60–64.

Retailing, although fragmented, is the backbone industry of Britain and 'one of the most dynamic and rapidly developing sectors of the UK economy' (James May, Director-General of the British Retail Consortium, 1996).

2 What is retailing?

Introduction

The basis of retailing is exchange. Money is exchanged for products (often called goods or merchandise) and services. Customers satisfy their needs with products for which they pay money to the retailer.

This book is about retailers and the products they sell, such as food, clothing or furnishings; goods that we can eat or wear or use in some way or another. It includes back-up services related to the selling of products, such as repair and credit services and telling a customer how a product works. Other forms of retailing include mail order through catalogues, magazines and television, and direct sales by salespeople calling at your home, but these areas are outside the scope of this book. Two factors are common to all areas of retailing: the buying and selling of goods and services, and dealing with people.

The chain of production

Retailing is part of the chain of production and distribution along which all products flow before they reach their ultimate destination: the consumer. On page 5 there is a diagram which shows the usual chain of events. Other systems have evolved, however, which suit the needs of particular products or markets. Some farm products may go direct from the farm to the retailer and many manufacturers deliver to large retailers direct. Nevertheless, despite the trend to merge the four links of the chain, the services which are usually provided to the consumer by the retailer have to be maintained. For example, it has always been the job of the retailer to operate the vital function of breaking down products sold in bulk (by the wholesaler) and selling them in small amounts to the consumer. It has proved difficult for other links of the production and distribution chain to take on this activity.

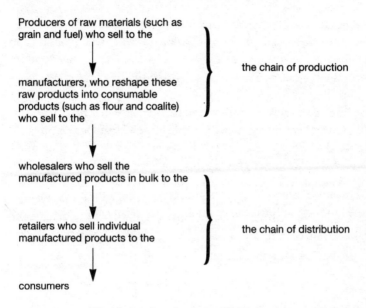

Producers of raw materials (such as grain and fuel) who sell to the

manufacturers, who reshape these raw products into consumable products (such as flour and coalite) who sell to the

the chain of production

wholesalers who sell the manufactured products in bulk to the

retailers who sell individual manufactured products to the

the chain of distribution

consumers

The chain of production and distribution

The activities of a retailer

The retailer who sells goods to the consumer is involved in many activities, each of which demands different skills and different amounts of time. In a small organisation, the activities will be taken on by one or two people only, but in a large organisation there may be many thousands of people involved in the various activities.

A retailer has to make efficient exchanges of money and goods to satisfy the needs of consumers and to make a profit, and the customer has to be provided with the products he or she requires.

The price of the product has to be low enough for the customer to want to buy, and high enough to ensure a profit. The retailer has to make sure that the goods are received and sold fast and easily, so the location of the stores, and of the goods within the stores, is of great importance. Promotion has to be sufficient for the consumer to have heard about the shop and its products through advertisements, window displays and the outside of the shop itself. The retailer also has to be concerned with the staff in the shop, and has to see that they are well treated, well paid and well looked after. Without staff who work well, no shop will function. So retailing is about the three Ps: people, prices and products, and it is the successful interaction of the three that makes for a successful business.

Shops are hardly ever restricted to one particular product. Usually, several or many items can be bought from one store. By stocking a large quantity of goods of considerable variety, in order to give the consumer choice, the retailer is taking on risks which the consumer does not have to bear. There may be some products which the retailer has bought and which are then not sold because of, for example, seasonal variations or fashion. The retailer will then be left with unsold stock which it may be possible to get rid of through sales, when goods are sold off at bargain prices.

Types of shop

There are at present around 340,000 shops in Britain. They may be of various kinds: a department store (such as Harrods in London), a multiple store (such as a branch of Dixons), a variety chain store (such as a branch of Marks and Spencer), a co-operative (such as a branch of the Co-operative Retail Services Society), a superstore (such as a branch of Sainsbury's), a hypermarket (such as one of the 14 Savacentres) or an independent store (such as the shop 'on the corner'). There are very large companies, operating over a thousand branches with many thousands of staff, and there are shops run by only two people.

There has been a marked decline in the total number of retail outlets over the last 20 years because many small independent stores have closed down. There has, however, been an increase in the number of superstores and hypermarkets (unknown 30 years ago) and large well-known companies have opened many big branches. This has meant fewer firms, each selling a greater volume of goods.

Conclusion

If you are interested in retailing, you would be more likely to find a job in a large firm than in an independent store. Working in a large store has many advantages. There is a wider selection of jobs, and there will also be better chances of promotion to positions of responsibility. Large retailers have been getting larger and their newer premises are mini-businesses in their own right. Large companies are also more likely to provide more benefits than small ones, such as: staff discount on goods, pension schemes, medical treatment and sickness benefits, subsidised meals, sports and other social facilities, educational schemes and personal insurance. However, there are also advantages in working for a small firm. It is far easier to get to know the customers and the rest of the staff, and the distance you travel to work will probably be far less.

Whatever company you choose to work for, you will be expected to work for long, possibly unsocial, hours. And you will also certainly be expected to work on Saturday, which is still the busiest trading day for most shops.

New Sunday trading laws started in 1994. They allow for stores of not more than 280 square metres to open at any time on Sunday. Stores over 280 square metres can open for six hours, any time between the hours of 10 a.m. and 6 p.m. Nobody is obliged to work on a Sunday for any reason whatsoever, but if an employee does agree to work on Sundays and signs a contract to do so, three months' notice is then required to contract out. Payment is negotiable; there is no set rate.

Also in 1994 the new Deregulation and Contracting Out Act came into being. This means that stores can trade at any time of the day or night (apart from Sundays). This has led to many outlets providing 24-hour opening times. Whatever hours are worked, these are subject to the usual employment laws, that is, a contractual agreement between two parties.

You can read more about the recent new trading regulations in Chapter 6 in the section on employment law, pages 62–64.

The range of jobs in retailing is enormous. There are many jobs available on a part-time basis, and because the new trading laws have resulted in longer opening hours, part-time work in retailing is increasing dramatically as there has been a noticeable trend towards shift work since the 1994 legislative changes. These changes may well suit women with young children, students, or other people who are unable to work full time. Almost all the jobs are interesting and many people cannot imagine working in any industry other than retailing as they find they have an absorbing commitment to their work.

3 The structure of the retailing industry

Department stores

In the mid-nineteenth century, stores such as Au Bon Marché in Paris and Bainbridge's in Newcastle introduced new shopping concepts, developed from the bazaars (covered markets) which were very popular in the early part of that century. They had many departments, where it was said that anything might be sold 'from a pin to an elephant'. Goods were offered with marked prices only, instead of allowing the practice of individual bargaining which was prevalent at the time. Anyone could enter these shops and look around without being obliged to buy anything. Customers had the right to exchange goods and have their money refunded and, because purchases were made on a large scale, goods could be sold at bargain prices. These shops were the first department stores.

The department store today may be thought of as a number of shops under one roof, a collection of selling departments in each of which retailing is carried out on a relatively small scale. It may specialise in a few kinds of goods or it may offer a large variety. A department store is also likely to have restaurant facilities.

Staff in department stores

Each store will have a manager for each department, usually known as a departmental manager. They will probably be experts in their particular lines of trading as they may be buyers as well as sellers of goods. Usually, however, they are not involved so much with the buying as with the selling and organisation of the particular department with which they are concerned.

In some stores there may be a chief buyer whom the various departmental managers have to consult before making their purchases. In other stores, buying and selling are separated and the buying department is a separate entity. As the turnover of a department store is large, buying must also be on a large scale. Purchases may be related to sales, and stocks may have to be sold before new supplies can be taken in. (The advantages of bulk buying may be passed on to the customers, who obtain better quality merchandise at a lower price.) As well as dealing direct with suppliers close to the stores, buyers may have to travel to different parts of the country and abroad.

Under the departmental managers are the supervisors who are in control of people selling the goods to the customers. The supervisors have to see that the assistants serve the customers properly, and keep their counters, shelves and stock in order. The sales assistants will usually be given training to cope with the modern techniques of selling. Training will alternate between periods of attendance on courses and practical work in the store.

Because the department store has to have a large turnover in order to survive, it has to seek a big market. Also, competition between the department store multiples and variety chain stores is increasing. Therefore, window display and advertising play a key part in the activities of a department store. Many jobs, involving extensive training, are available in this field.

Altogether, an average department store is likely to have over 400 staff, including plumbers, painters, dressmakers, display and security staff. Training schemes are attached to most shop-floor jobs, and there are usually clearly defined promotional paths.

Two examples of department stores, the way they function, the jobs they carry and their training courses are set out below.

PROFILE: Fenwick Ltd

Fenwick Ltd is a group of successful department stores. A family-owned business, it was started in Newcastle in 1882 by Mr John James Fenwick, who concentrated originally on ladies' tailoring. Today, although there are many selling departments, ladies' fashion is the major retailing area. There are now (1997) eight stores:

- *Bond Street* has a staff of 200 and is concerned largely with women's fashion. There are also two restaurants, including Joe's, a menswear department, hairdressing and a cards and gift department.
- *Brent Cross* has a staff of 650 with a wide range of merchandise, as well as a hairdressing department and two restaurants.
- *Canterbury*, where Fenwick has taken over Riceman's department store.
- *Leicester* has a staff of 300, a wide range of merchandise, a hairdressing department and two restaurants.
- *Newcastle* is the largest store, with a staff of 1,200. The departments cover a wide range of merchandise and there is a hair and beauty salon, as well as five restaurants.
- *Windsor* is a small store with about 55 staff, a hairdressing department and a restaurant.
- *York* has a staff of about 200. There are children's wear, hairdressing, cookshops and toy departments. There is also a Man's Shop and a restaurant.
- *Tunbridge Wells* is the second custom-built store, employing around 250 staff in a variety of fashion departments, menswear, gifts and one restaurant.

Career development at Fenwick

The initial aim of your career will be to reach the position of buyer. Progress to this position is usually rapid – the average age on appointment is 24–25 years.

After gaining experience in a number of departments as part of your training, your first significant promotion will be to underbuyer or section manager. Your main task will be the day-to-day running of the department, deputising for the buyer, who is often away from the store. You will take responsibility for selling operations, customer relations, organisation and development of staff, stock control and presentation. Working closely with the buyer, you will have plenty of scope for implementing your ideas and developing your role within the store. From here, you will progress to buyer, responsible for the profitable management of your department. You will be selecting merchandise and will travel in the UK and possibly abroad. You will manage the sales staff, and when in the store you will lead the selling team. Success in your first buyership will mean promotion to buying for a larger department.

There are a variety of ways in which a successful buyer's career can develop, depending on individual strengths and abilities. Some buyers progress to merchandise manager, responsible to the merchandise director for implementing the store's overall trading policy. It is also possible to develop the buying role, taking on increased responsibility in more than one store.

Working with Fenwick

All staff have the same basic terms and conditions of employment, but some variations do occur between stores, for example, in starting salary and in the pattern of working hours. All staff share the following:

◆ Five-day working week with every other Saturday free
◆ Staff discount of 20 per cent after a qualifying period
◆ Discretionary bonus, based on length of service
◆ Four weeks' holiday entitlement, rising to five weeks
◆ Staff pension and life assurance schemes
◆ Subsidised meals.

Training schemes

There are two main routes to a buyership with the Fenwick training schemes: the Graduate Training Scheme and the Management Training Scheme for school leavers.

Graduate Training Scheme

A Graduate Training Scheme is available at Newcastle, Brent Cross and Bond Street, starting in early September. While Fenwick does consider graduates from any discipline, a business studies or textile-related course is preferable. The aim of the scheme is to give an insight into the company and the individual store, an understanding of the buyer's job, and training in how to manage people. The programmes differ to some extent in each store, but all share the following key elements:

- Induction course, giving an introduction to directors and senior management and an explanation of the main store functions
- Selling experience in several departments
- Developing an understanding of all store systems
- Project work, usually in conjunction with a buyer, merchandise manager or director
- Attachments to all main non-selling areas
- Instruction in management skills and retail law
- Discussions on trainees' progress with their merchandise manager, staff manager and store director.

Positions of responsibility are given at an early stage. Graduates are expected to be ready for their first promotion to buyer's clerk/merchandise administrator within 12 months and, if successful, could become buyers within three to five years.

Management Training Scheme

Some Fenwick stores run a Management Training Scheme for school leavers. You can apply if you are 18 years old and have, or expect to get, at least two A-levels at grade C or above or a BTEC Higher National pass or above. The scheme begins in August or early September and lasts for up to two years. The aim of the scheme is to train the buyers and managers of the future by giving them an insight into how the business is run, broadening their commercial knowledge and preparing them for their first supervisory position. The main components of the scheme include:

- ◆ Training sessions with directors, merchandise managers and buyers, covering all aspects of the store's activities
- ◆ Supervisory and related courses, possibly with day release
- ◆ Departmental placements with instruction from buyers
- ◆ Experience in several different departments selling a variety of merchandise
- ◆ Attachments to the non-selling departments of the store
- ◆ Regular assessment of progress by the buyer and staff manager.

Application must be made direct to the store you want to work in.

Further information can be obtained from Fenwick of Bond Street Ltd, New Bond Street, London W1A 3BS.

PROFILE: The John Lewis Partnership Department Stores

John Lewis maintain their achievement is built on the factor that makes the real difference: people. They strongly believe that the people who make the profit should also share in the profit, so that all staff are partners. They should also have a big say in how the company is run and the right to question top management if they think the business is not performing. In short, everyone is accountable in a successful and democratic business.

The Partnership offers competitive salaries with financial benefits that include free life assurance, non-contributory pensions, substantial shopping discounts and the use of leisure facilities. Each year every partner receives a share of the profits expressed as a percentage of pay (20 per cent in 1997).

Management Development Programme

The retailing business is highly competitive and fast-moving. Managers have to be sound in judgement and quick to respond to changing conditions. They have to be people with the desire and potential to take on responsibility, and meet the challenge of leading and motivating others.

John Lewis look for people from all kinds of backgrounds, with different personalities and ambitions; school leavers with A-levels, those with proven experience in retail management or individuals wishing to switch from their current careers to retailing, as well as people able to resume a career after a time away from work.

The programme is designed to equip you with the skills you need to take that first step into the management structure, as a section manager. That means being in charge of a section within a department. If you show particular ability in the role, you will have the opportunity to progress to the level of department manager, with sole responsibility for running a department and managing a team.

The programme is completely flexible and will be tailored to individual needs. So the length of your particular programme depends on factors such as your experience and ability. Promotion from the scheme to the position of section manager and beyond depends on your proven ability to perform the tasks required and show concrete evidence of the personal qualities and management skills required.

John Lewis also recruit school leavers with GCSEs to study for the NVQ in retailing Levels 1 and 2.

For further information write to the Staff Manager of the John Lewis Department Store nearest to you.

Graduate Training Scheme

John Lewis look for qualities in graduate recruits such as the ability to lead and work well in a team, along with commitment, enthusiasm and high standards of personal presentation. The aim is to capitalise on each individual's strengths and qualities.

Running a department in a John Lewis Department Store is, in many ways, like running your own business: a business you could be managing within two years of leaving university, thanks to the wide-ranging training programme.

For the first two years you will work in one specific department store. Involvement in the day-to-day running of a department, as well as on-the-job training, will be supported by regular tutorials, seminars and residential courses at the company Management Training Centre. Promotion to department manager will probably involve moving to another department store. Mobility will be essential for your future, allowing you to take up promotion opportunities as they arise. From there you can choose whether to specialise in areas such as buying or personnel, or set your sights on becoming a managing director, the head of a department store. Talent and ability alone dictate the scope and progress of your career.

For further information write to the Head of Management Development, John Lewis Partnership, 171 Victoria Street, London SW1E 5NN.

Multiples

Multiples are companies with at least ten, and usually many more, branches in different areas of the country which stock a number of specialist products. Some of the biggest multiples have well over 1,000 branches.

The first multiple company was Singer (the sewing machine group) which had a network of 160 shops in 1871. Other multiples in the nineteenth century included Freeman Hardy and Willis (the shoe specialists), Burtons (the men's clothing specialists) and the Home and Colonial Stores. Methods of mass production at that time were becoming ever more efficient, and that meant distribution also had to be managed on a larger scale. This in turn led to multiple branch retailing through regional outlets. Today, two large specialist fields for multiples are electrical retailing and photographic and audio equipment.

The various branch shops of multiples are under the control of a head office and are operated as a company under a board of directors and a general manager who will normally take responsibility for the central departments at head office. Larger multiples, with over 60 branches, appoint district (or area) managers who are each in charge of a regional group of branches. If there are 1,000 or more branches, there can be up to 40 district managers who may be responsible to up to four area managers, who, in turn, are responsible to the director of the company. Each shop is under the control of a branch (or store) manager who may be quite remote from the people working at the organisation's headquarters. Here it might be noted that the branch manager will not do the buying; this is centralised at head office.

Computers help to streamline the recording of cash receipts. This makes the daily checking of cash and stock a relatively easy operation, and means that returns to head office can be made very quickly. Branch accounts are always kept at head office. Usually, the branches possess identical shop fronts, so that they may be recognised immediately by the public. Merchandise sold in one branch compares in range and quality with that in other branches, and prices tend to be uniform throughout. Planning, stock control, distribution, laboratory testing, work study, statistics, research, personnel, sales promotion, legal and security departments will all be housed at head office, from whence instructions flow to branches.

Multiples operate at low costs because of their bulk buying. By buying in bulk quantities there will almost certainly be extra discounts from suppliers, who may well offer additional advantages in terms and conditions. Specialist managers and staff will be employed to look after the buying, accounting, training, personnel, display, site location, work study, advertising and shop layout. Low costs also operate on account of modern merchandising techniques and standard merchandising. Large quantities of merchandise can be bought and sold, with price tags printed in bulk, staff interchanged, and national advertising campaigns brought into operation on account of standardisation of the products. It is also easy to transfer stock from one shop to another.

There are, however, some problems that face multiples. Administrative costs are high because of the need to operate a large head office and a network of supervisors. There is usually the need for a fair amount of advertising, and this is always very expensive. As control stems from head office, branch managers cannot use much initiative. This may mean that some shops are not operating efficiently. For example, they may not be selling the right products in a particular area because head office has not taken note of the area's particular needs at a particular time. Nevertheless, even though one branch may be doing bad business, the drop in business in one area will not usually affect the company as a whole unduly because there are many branches spread over the country, which means that the risks of the enterprise as a whole are spread.

Many multiples are part of large national and multinational organisations. An example of one such is given below.

PROFILE: The Museum Company

The Company was founded in 1989 and the first store opened in the same year in the Fashion Centre at Pentagon City, Washington DC. By mid-1995 the Company had 67 stores in the USA and Canada and franchises in Japan and Korea. Expansion into the UK started in 1995 with stores opening at Brent Cross in north London and Kingston in south London in November 1995. Stores stock art reproductions from museums around the world. Further stores are planned to open in the UK in late 1997 and 1998.

Assistants working in the stores have intensive training sessions every Saturday morning for up to an hour at a time. They are trained to talk to people and are given a thorough grounding in communication skills. They are also taught about the stock they sell and the artists who created the originals. Additionally, they are given training in self-esteem, to help them feel confident and self-assured in dealing with customers.

Variety chain stores

Variety chain stores are large shops that sell a wide range of goods. The stock in one company's many hundreds of shops is limited to goods which sell quickly, needing the minimum sales service. So in these shops the customer will not usually be able to try on clothes or ask a sales assistant how a particular product works. Items are displayed and priced so that the customer can examine them without calling upon the assistant's time, except for wrapping the product bought and taking the money. Personal service is thus cut down to a minimum. Most of the merchandise is priced as low as possible, and prices tend to be the same throughout all branches in one particular company.

All branches of the company will have the same outside layout (to make the shops easily identifiable to the customer), the same variety of goods and a similar interior layout. However, the counter location for some of the goods may be changed frequently and 'impulse' purchases, such as confectionery and cosmetics, are often placed near entrances or exits. (For example, it has long been a policy in Woolworth stores to place a confectionery 'pick 'n mix' counter near the entrance, with the stated aim of attracting young customers who are less likely to penetrate deep into the shops.)

There has recently been a trend towards credit and delivery, and some organisations (for example, Marks and Spencer) offer their own credit facilities. Central buying is the general rule, and buyers hold positions of great responsibility because of the enormous amount of merchandise stocked and sold. There is a close liaison between the firms and the many manufacturers who supply them. Brand names are frequently used; for example, Marks and Spencer use the name 'St Michael' on all their products.

The numerous branch shops are controlled by head office and are operated as a company under a board of directors and a general manager. Each store is controlled by a manager and assistant managers, together with supervisors who organise the sales staff.

A brief account of a variety chain store is given below, together with descriptions of some of the jobs and training schemes provided. The range of jobs is very wide, so only a few can be outlined.

PROFILE: W H Smith Group plc

In 1792 Henry Walton Smith opened a news agency in London. His wife, Anna, ran it for 24 years after his death, but it was his son, William Henry Smith, who expanded the business. He saw a potential for the railway station bookstall where, as well as books and newspapers, he sold candles to read by and blankets for the passengers to keep themselves warm. Over the last 80 years the chain has moved into the high street; currently there are around 500 retail branches, including airport, station and hospital book-shops.

The W H Smith Group comprises W H Smith, Waterstone's Booksellers, Virgin Our Price, W H Smith News and W H Smith USA. The Group employs nearly 35,000 people in the UK and USA.

W H Smith Retail

Approximately 14,000 staff are employed in W H Smith Retail, many of whom work part time. There is comprehensive training at all levels and all employees acquire the expertise to make a full contribution to the retail team. Training for extra qualifications is also offered, such as the NVQ in Retailing at Level 2 (see page 70). For those keen to progress, two programmes are offered, the Department Management Programme and the Retail Management Development Programme.

Further information is available from the manager of any W H Smith branch.

Waterstone's Booksellers

Waterstone's is the leading specialist bookseller in the UK and Ireland with over 100 bookshops. Virtually all positions above entry level are recruited internally. It is a highly decentralised company, with most training taking place at branch level.

Skills and development training are offered to managers and assistant managers. A formal booksellers' development pro-gramme is currently being developed.

Further information is available from your local Waterstone's bookshop, or from the Personnel Director, Waterstone's Book-sellers, Capital Court, Capital Interchange Way, Brentford, Mid-dlesex TW8 0EX.

Virgin Our Price

Following three years of continued expansion, Virgin Our Price now has over 300 stores nationwide and has long been established as one of the leading music and entertainment retailers in the world. The company operates a policy of encouraging internal promotion with opportunities in stores and at head office being advertised in each business unit on a weekly basis. This enables the majority of head office vacancies to be filled from within the business. Recruitment decisions within the business are based purely on the grounds of a candidate's relevant skills and experience.

On joining the business, each new employee has the opportunity to work with a comprehensive retail training framework, known as Entertainment Retail Skills (ERS). The framework offers on-going training and enables employees not only to learn and develop according to their present roles but also offers opportunities for people to develop and learn more about other roles which in turn encourages multi-skilling within the store environment. The ERS framework consists of 12 modules and will prepare employees for progression within the store environment. It will also assist in an employee's development to a management position.

Once in a managerial position, each employee is then able to move on to the management training framework, Managing Your Development, which supports his or her continuing learning and development in the store management role. The emphasis at this stage is with each employee taking the initiative and responsibility for driving his or her own development and working with the business to facilitate learning.

Further information is available from the Career Planning and Recruitment Department, Virgin Our Price, Kew House, Capital Interchange Way, Brentford, Middlesex TW8 0EX.

Supermarkets, superstores and hypermarkets

This section is mostly concerned with the grocery sector and its main product, food. The grocery sector's main outlets are supermarkets, superstores and hypermarkets, which are usually categorised as follows:

Supermarkets	Superstores	Hypermarkets
2,000–25,000 sq ft	25,000–50,000 sq ft	Over 50,000 sq ft
Up to about 50 staff	50–250 staff	250 staff or more
but more likely 15–30		

Supermarkets

A supermarket normally has a minimum floor space of 2,000 sq ft. (A shop run on similar lines, but with less selling space than this is called a mini market.) There will be up to 50 staff, and at least three checkouts. Almost all the products will be pre-packed food.

Superstores

Superstores, which are found in towns and cities, particularly in shopping centres, employ a minimum of 50 staff and usually many more. They are predominantly grocery-based, although there are some companies, such as Tesco, which have up to 50 per cent of merchandise other than groceries.

Hypermarkets

A hypermarket is a very large store with at least 50,000 sq ft of selling space. Some are as large as two football pitches put together! They sell everything from furniture to food, usually on one level, at discount prices, and under one roof.

Hypermarkets are free-standing buildings, that is, they are located in isolation from any others, and are usually sited on the fringes of towns and cities, never in them. There are on-site warehousing facilities and car parking for over a thousand cars.

The goods sold are mainly on a cash and cheque and self-service basis, and customers can wheel their purchases to their cars on a trolley. There may, however, be delivery and credit arrangements for large and expensive items, normally at extra cost. The range of goods in hypermarkets is wider than that in supermarkets and superstores. For example, there will probably be wardrobes and hi-fi sets for sale. Hypermarkets operate on very low gross profit margins (about 12 per cent on food compared with about 16 per cent in supermarkets).

An example of a company with numerous branches involved primarily in the grocery sector is outlined below.

PROFILE: Waitrose Ltd

In 1937 the John Lewis Partnership acquired Waitrose, a small group of high-class grocery shops founded in 1904 by Wallace Waite, Arthur Rose and David Taylor. Today (1997) there are 110 Waitrose supermarkets, employing over 21,000 people throughout the south of England, East Anglia and the Midlands.

From the day you join Waitrose you become a partner of the John Lewis Partnership. The company is owned by those who work in it, so everyone on a permanent contract is effectively a co-owner. The Partnership's aim is to give all partners the opportunity of sharing as far as possible in the benefits and responsibilities of ownership. As a partner you have a say in the way the business is run through elected representatives on various councils. A major benefit is the annual partnership bonus; every year, after business investment has been made, all remaining profit is distributed to partners as a cash bonus. Other benefits include discount on most goods sold in the Partnership and a non-contributory pension scheme.

School leaver opportunities

Waitrose has developed a training scheme lasting 12 months for those leaving school aged 16. Trainees will have a sponsor to show them the ropes and act as a friend and guide. Everyone is different, so the programme is adapted to suit the trainee as an individual. Trainees will complete a series of work attachments in different sections of the shop, use self-study materials and acquire the many retail skills needed to set them on an exciting career.

A-level opportunities

The Retail Management Training Scheme starts in September each year and is open to candidates aged 17–22 who have studied to A-level standard. The programme prepares the trainee for a management position as a section manager within two years in a Waitrose supermarket. During the first stage of training the trainee will gain an overall view of how a Waitrose branch operates. The emphasis will be on learning how to organise and manage time. Over the two years the trainee will gradually take on additional responsibility for managing others.

In addition to on-the-job work experience, trainees will use self-study materials under the guidance of a department manager and attend review days when they will have the opportunity to meet other trainees and exchange ideas.

If the trainee successfully completes the two-year programme, there is an opportunity to continue training to become a department manager, a member of the senior branch management team, and to study for a Foundation Certificate in Management from the Institute of Grocery Distribution (see Chapters 9 and 10).

Management Training Scheme

Designed for experienced managers joining Waitrose, the scheme lasts between six and nine months and is made up of a series of work attachments in various Waitrose branches, practical work, and outside courses at management training centres. A specific programme is set up to meet the needs of each individual, taking experience and background into account. A management trainer is assigned to a group of trainees and regular performance reviews are held throughout the programme when progress is discussed with the trainee, the trainer and the manager.

Graduate Training Scheme

Graduates of any discipline can apply for entry. The training programme lasts between 18 and 22 months and includes work attachments in about five Waitrose branches, together with practical projects and formal training at the management training centre. Individual placements are also offered to undergraduates taking sandwich courses. The placement usually lasts 12 months, starting in August each year. Placement students are based at the head office, where there are opportunities in buying, food technology, IT, merchandising, packaging, distribution and accountancy. Related degree disciplines are required for all these areas.

For further information, write to The Staff Training Department, Waitrose Ltd, Southern Industrial Area, Bracknell, Berkshire RG12 8YA.

Retail co-operatives

Retail co-operatives are autonomous retail societies which function as a major part of the co-operative movement in the UK, and, added together, are the largest retailers in Europe. They are registered by the Registrar of Friendly Societies under the Industrial and Provident Societies Acts.

At the moment, there are about 50 retail co-operatives in the UK. The total membership is around 8 million and these societies run about 4,650 shops, including 90 superstores. Each society has its own management and career structure, and the largest publish their own careers literature. There is a wide range of jobs available within the retail co-operative sector (see the table on page 26). In 1997 around 80,000 people were employed by the retail societies. Nearly all employed are members of their appropriate trade unions, and wages are determined nationally by the Co-operative Employers' Association and the trade unions. A number of societies operate Youth Training Schemes.

Most of the early societies, such as the Rochdale Pioneers, supplied mainly groceries and other foodstuffs. Food and dairy supplies still account for about 70 per cent of the total retail society turnover. Most societies, however, also supply merchandise such as clothing, textiles, footwear, electrical, hardware, furniture, pharmaceuticals, optical and toilet requisites, cater for DIY and gardening enthusiasts, operate petrol stations and provide an extensive network of travel bureaux. The co-operative sector also arranges over 150,000 funerals annually.

Ideals and principles of the co-operative movement

The co-operative movement follows certain ideals and principles. One ultimate ideal is to achieve a more equitable distribution of wealth in the country, and people in the co-operative movement believe that their form of production and distribution will achieve this eventually. A more equitable distribution of wealth would help to raise the standard of living of the majority of people in Britain.

Food	*Head office*
Junior management trainees	Junior accounting trainees
Checkout operators	General clerks
Sales staff	Junior secretaries
Branch managers	Data control clerks
Area managers	Systems analyst trainees
	Computer operator trainees
	Personnel department trainees
Non-food	*Dairies*
Junior management trainees	Junior dairy assistants
Sales staff	Laboratory assistants
Section heads	
Display staff	
Stores offices (cashiers, investment clerks, etc.)	

Some of the many career opportunities for young men and women in retail co-operative societies

Co-operators believe that, in time, the co-operative movement could provide a complete alternative to private enterprise in production and distribution, and promote the formulation of a co-operative commonwealth.

Co-operative principles, originally established by the Rochdale Pioneers in 1844, and revised in 1966 by the 23rd Congress of the International Co-operative Alliance, are:

1. Open membership. This means that in Britain anyone over the age of 16 can become a member by buying one or more £1 shares.
2. Democratic ownership and control – one member, one vote. (Regardless of the amount of share capital or the amount of purchases made, each member has one vote only.)
3. Payment of limited interest on capital.
4. The surplus of profit of a society to be distributed to members in proportion to their trade with the society or used for development of the business of the co-operative or the provision of common services.
5. Provision of education for members, officers, employees and the general public.
6. Co-operation among co-operators nationally and internationally.

Structure of the co-operative movement

Members of a retail society are recruited from the general public. They elect a board of directors which appoints a chief officer and senior staff to manage the business of a co-operative, which may include branches and specialist departments. Supplies come from the Co-operative Wholesale Society (CWS) (see below) and direct from the manufacturers. The retail societies and the CWS finance the Co-operative Union (see below) which is the movement's adviser, co-ordinator and mouthpiece; it directs the educational department of the co-operative movement and the Co-operative College (see below).

The Co-operative Wholesale Society (CWS)

The CWS, founded in 1863 to serve the needs of consumer co-operatives, is Britain's largest co-operative retailer with more than 700 stores in the UK. Employing around 40,000 people, it remains the co-operative movement's largest supplier and is Britain's largest commercial farmer, responsible for 45,000 acres of land. It is also a major food manufacturer and is the largest UK-owned funeral director.

The CWS is owned by retail societies and individual shoppers who elect its board of 35 directors. Major CWS subsidiaries include the Co-operative Bank, which has 1.5 million customer accounts, and the Co-operative Insurance Society, one of Britain's largest insurance organisations.

Retail Co-op branches of the CWS include Scottish, South East, Greater Nottingham, Cumbrian, South Midlands, North Eastern, Belfast, Enfield, St Albans, and Milton Keynes. The CWS is also a major shareholder in National Co-operative Chemists with 200 branches, and Shoefayre, the footwear retailer, which has 220 branches.

Retail job applicants should in the first instance contact the regional CWS retail branches.

Co-operative Retail Services

Co-operative Retail Services (CRS), or Co-operative as it is also known, has about 1.5 million members and employs some 25,000 staff in about 550 outlets around the country. There is a comprehensive staff training programme for all staff employed by the CRS.

The organisation was formed in 1934 with a view to setting up shops in areas lacking co-operative facilities, but subsequently it started absorbing retail societies in economic difficulties and likely to close. To date, the CRS has incorporated some 200 formerly independent societies, including the London Co-operative Society which merged with the CRS in February 1981. Co-operative is controlled by a board of directors elected by CRS regional committees. The Society's food business operates supermarkets and superstores as well as convenience stores. Its supermarkets and superstores will soon be harmonised under the Co-operative Pioneer fascia and its convenience stores are to be known as Co-operative Locals. The flagships of the non-food business are its 50plus departmental stores which are business co-operative Living stores and the seven Co-operative Home-world out-of-town durable superstores. The Society also provides extensive funeral services, as well as petrol stations and TV rentals.

The CRS board of directors appoints a chief executive officer who is directly responsible to the board for the trading and financial operations of the society. Each of the divisions within CRS has a national manager who is supported by a managerial, secretarial and clerical team.

Other societies

The other societies which make up the co-operative movement vary enormously in size. Some have only one store, while others have 500 or so. The typical profile will be a central department store and offices in the main town or city; increasingly, however, the trend is towards the operation of major hypermarkets and superstores, often on the outskirts, which provide a comprehensive range of services (credit, banking, travel, restaurant, etc) in addition to normal self-service facilities.

There are around 2,500 smaller food units and over 1,000 non-food units which cater for consumers in the suburbs and neighbouring towns and villages.

Details of careers and appointments within these societies can be obtained for the Societies' Head Offices, the addresses of which can be found in Yellow Pages.

The Co-operative Union

The Co-operative Union is the national federation of consumer co-operative societies in Britain and was established in 1969. It is controlled by the retail societies and the CWS, and is the overall co-ordinating body for their activities. The Co-operative Union provides advisory services, such as financial and legal advice, and up-to-date political and commercial information. It also acts as the co-operative representative on government bodies and other public and private organisations. Through the Co-operative Union, societies consider national problems and frame national and international policies at an annual national congress. The Co-operative Union runs the Co-operative College (see below) and an education department, both located at Stanford Hall near Loughborough, which provide services and courses to societies in staff training and education of the Society's members and lay members.

The Co-operative College

The Co-operative College Trust is an educational charity established in 1944 as a centenary memorial to the Rochdale Pioneers. It is an international management training school and community education residential centre.

The college's educational services division offers trade association courses for members of the Co-operative Union, and generally promotes the development of staff education and training and member education. This programme includes short intensive courses mainly in specialised aspects of co-operative management. There is a considerable variety of courses, including advanced study courses in management.

Specialist international courses include postgraduate Diploma courses in co-operative development and management, co-operative accountancy and financial management, co-operative education and training and co-operative financial services.

The College provides a Diploma in policy studies and this is dedicated to three specific subject areas: the environment, British heritage and Europe 2000. Each course lasts for approximately six months on a residential basis, and there is in addition an extended essay which is to be completed in the student's own time, but within six months of the residential period. The Diploma is accepted by most universities as evidence of suitability for entry to higher education.

The Co-operative College also offers training schemes for graduates.

The College runs a unique Discovery Learning Programme for youth trainees leading to the Retail Industry Capability Certificate. Audio tapes, projects and work-based assignments are a feature of this programme, which places the responsibility for learning on the trainees themselves.

Another division of the College, the CLEAR unit, provides a worldwide research and consultancy service. The unit currently manages projects in the UK and in developing countries.

A recent innovation for the retail industry has been the Consortium of Retail Teaching Companies, based at the College, which includes major retailing companies such as Boots, Marks and Spencer, Sainsbury, Dixons, Asda, Kingfisher and Argyll. The Consortium provides an intensive programme of work experience and training for undergraduates.

Management courses

Courses are organised by the College for all levels of retail management. Such courses include management skills and management techniques, a six-month graduate retail management training scheme and specialist training for bank staff and managers in the funeral service.

The College also offers a Diploma in Management Studies and has developed an MBA programme suitable for students from the UK and abroad.

Further information can be obtained from: The Director of Studies, The Co-operative College Ltd, Stanford Hall, Loughborough, Leicestershire LE13 5QH.

Independents

Independent firms are generally regarded as organisations with fewer than ten branches. The shops are usually small and tend to be owned by one person, who may employ members of his or her family and sometimes a few assistants, so careers in this area of retailing are limited. A number of the employees may work part time, so that there are enough people to serve when the shop is busy without having assistants waiting around when trade is slack. Even so, many people want to run their own business, which can be a challenging and exciting occupation with excellent prospects. A wide range of skills is needed to manage a small shop as, apart from managing the business, the manager is also responsible for the welfare and training of staff and the security of the stock and premises.

Independents have many advantages over larger concerns. The small shop may be more conveniently sited, and much more personal attention is usually given to the customer, who may therefore be more satisfied. A delivery service may be available. There may be greater flexibility in operating the store, and much less capital is needed to start a small business.

There are some disadvantages, however. The small shop cannot always be stocked with a large amount of merchandise and so the choice of goods may be limited, and there may be a lack of storage space. If the turnover is slow, the independent shopkeeper will have to keep some of the stock for a long time, and it may deteriorate. The goods may have to be offered at higher prices than those at larger stores because sales volume will not attract discounts from suppliers. Also, the small retailer often cannot afford the best sites in town because of high rates and rents.

To show the diversity of merchandise sold in the independent sector, a few areas relevant to independents are described below.

Confectionery, tobacco and newspapers

These shops, known as CTNs, sell mainly newspapers, confectionery (sweets and chocolate) and cigarettes, but other items are also available such as ice-creams, cards, stationery, books and other food items. There are currently (1997) around 30,000 such shops in the UK.

There are no specific qualifications for people wishing to enter the trade, either as a sales assistant or as an assistant manager. For further information contact the National Federation of Retail Newsagents (see page 83).

Fashion

Fashion shops cater for men's, women's and girls' clothing. The majority of the staff are sales assistants who serve customers, check stock and often help out with window displays. No particular qualifications are needed, though there are courses on how to become a sales assistant in this field. The most convenient way of getting a job may be to walk into a fashion shop and ask whether there are any jobs available.

Jewellery

The jewellery trade falls largely into two categories: shops which sell a wide variety of goods suitable for gifts, and shops which specialise in one or more section of the trade, such as silver (modern or antique), jewellery, watches or clocks, or bespoke pieces.

Assistants need to know about the qualities of the jewels they sell. They have to understand how modern clocks and watches work, and why they vary in price. They may also have to know about hallmarks on silverware, or deal with valuation and repair enquiries.

A young trainee employed by a firm with a number of shops can expect to move from one local branch to another as his or her career progresses.

Behind-the-scenes trainee craftspeople are often required for the repair of jewellery and watches, and there have been many instances of craftspeople, as well as sales staff, going on to open their own businesses.

Basic educational requirements vary from firm to firm. Some may recruit school leavers with GCSE qualifications, while others may be more interested in young people with the right attitudes, personality and enthusiasm.

Examination courses are run by the National Association of Goldsmiths, the Gemmological Association and Gem Testing Laboratory of Great Britain, and the British Horological Institute (see Chapters 9 and 10). There are also BTEC and SCOTVEC examinations applicable to the jewellery trade.

Pharmacy

Pharmacies provide jobs for many sales assistants, dispensing technicians and pharmacists.

The main function of a retail pharmacy is to supply drugs and medicines. By law, there always has to be a pharmacist on duty when the shop is open. In addition to medicines, most pharmacies stock a wide range of other goods, including cosmetics, perfumes and baby-care products. The newly qualified pharmacist will find there are a large number of independent businesses, each owned and run by a single pharmacist.

A dispensing technician works under the supervision of the retail pharmacist. Usually this means helping the pharmacist to prepare and dispense medicines, check stock and carry out clerical tasks. In many pharmacies the technician also assists with sales over the counter.

As a sales assistant you will help in the day-to-day work in the shop, selling and advising the customer, pricing the goods, restocking the shelves, and putting away goods when they come in from suppliers.

For further information and details of courses, see Chapters 9 and 10, and contact the Royal Pharmaceutical Society.

4 Jobs in retailing and career opportunities

Sales staff and shelf-fillers

Personal qualities, rather than educational qualifications, are important for sales staff, who are the people who serve the customers and who probably have the most varied of all jobs in retailing. You need to be smartly dressed, be able to talk easily, and have a reasonable knowledge of arithmetic. In particular, you need to know about the customers, the products sold and the methods of selling. The jobs of sales staff vary very widely. For example, there is a great difference between selling furniture, where staff may only see a few customers a day and where each sale is for a large amount of money, and selling newspapers or sweets in a newsagent's shop, where there is a steady stream of people all day long spending small amounts.

The success of a store depends to a very large extent on the attitudes and social skills of sales staff. If you want to sell goods to customers, courtesy and an ability to get on with all types of people are essential qualities. You will have to greet and recognise different customers, and you must also be prepared to interest them and discover their needs. You have to judge customers' motives for buying and show them suitable stock. You will have to advise customers on the suitability of their purchases and, at the same time, make sure that the goods are sold. You are responsible for making a sale and suggesting other sales to the same customer, if possible. It will be necessary to collect payment from the customer and give the correct change and receipts.

Stock levels have to be checked constantly and stock replaced when necessary. You have to make sure that stock is tidy, well presented and priced correctly, and that stock lists are made. You have to advise on faulty stock and on the style, quality and properties of the merchandise. In off-peak hours you will be involved in helping the display staff with both window and internal displays. You also have to look after your own department and make sure that that, too, is clean and tidy.

With certain types of merchandise you need to have some knowledge of the products, and some skills may be necessary to explain to the customers how they work. Sales work provides essential training for higher level posts such as supervisors, managers, or buyers.

Training

Entry qualifications and further education and training for sales staff vary from company to company. Some shops only recruit school leavers with good GCSE passes. Others look for people with personality, a will to work hard and a reasonable standard of English and maths. There are the Business and Technology Education Council (BTEC) foundation GNVQs or Scottish Vocational Education Council (SCOTVEC) awards available for school leavers with no academic qualifications if they can satisfy the particular college that they are sufficiently competent in English to make satisfactory progress, and the National Vocational Qualification (NVQ) in Retailing. (For further information about these courses, see Chapter 9.)

Case Study

Paul is 16 and works as a sales assistant in the showroom of a builder's merchant.

'It's all part of a four-year apprenticeship. I began in the stockroom where I spent four months learning about the store's procedure and the products we sell. When I've finished here, I'll probably go on to the paint shop for a spell, then the electrical counter, and so on. I've set up a number of kitchen and bathroom displays. It gives me the opportunity to put my ideas into practice, but I've got to accept criticism when things go wrong.'

Although his firm has trade departments, most of the people in the showroom are ordinary shoppers, and an important part of Paul's job is dealing with their problems, finding out what they really want and selling them something appropriate to their needs.

Checkout operators

Checkout operators (also known as cashiers, cashout operators or till assistants) work in supermarkets, freezer centres and most self-service stores. Their job is to ring up customer purchases on a cash register or till. Most cash registers not only show different types of merchandise but also calculate change. Some keyboards show subtotals so that a customer is able to ask at any point how much money has been spent. Most tills in supermarkets now read the bar codes electronically to help checkout operators with their work. A checkout operator also has to know how to deal with cheques, debit cards, credit cards and customer accounts.

In supermarkets, checkout operators are sometimes the only people employed who are seen by the customers, and it is there-fore very important that they are efficient and helpful. During quiet periods, operators often help out with other jobs such as shelf filling. They will probably have to work on Saturdays, but will get compensations such as staff discounts and days off during the week.

Training

Training is carried out in the supermarket or self-service store, usually by qualified instructors. During their training, checkout operators learn that there is more to the job than appears at first sight. They have to be trained about security and what to do in cases of suspected shoplifting, and also have to learn to deal with certain problems, such as when shoppers do not have enough money to pay the bill, which involves the cancellation of receipts and sales records.

Case Study

Lisa works in a supermarket as a checkout operator. Before she starts work in the morning she makes sure her checkout is clean, that there is a receipt roll in her till, and that she has enough plastic bags. She also takes a quick look around the store before the customers come in to see if there are any price changes or special offers.

When customers queue up at the checkout, Lisa takes each item from the basket and rings it up on the till. Goods such as butter and cheese have to be put into bags, and she has separate keys to press for fish, meat, fruit and vegetables, and general items such as washing powder or cooking oil. Coding the items correctly is very important because, by doing so, Lisa programmes the till to record the sales figures for each department so that it is known whether or not trade has improved. She does not have to worry about the change as the till is computerised and will indicate how much money to give to the customer.

'I thought I knew all about shop life and was surprised when I had to do a week's training when I started here. I thought it was a bit unnecessary until I went on a till. There are lots of procedures – such as what items should be put in bags and dealing with cheques and money-off coupons. Even the way you give the change and receipt can be important when you come up against an awkward customer.'

Display staff

Well-designed window displays and displays inside the stores are essential to attract customers and encourage them to make a purchase. In small shops the display is the responsibility of the manager, and it is undertaken by experienced shop assistants who have shown a flair for the job. In large department stores and multiples, however, there is usually a full-time display team headed by a manager. Multiple stores usually have a central studio team designing standard displays for production in all the windows and interiors. This team will have a busy time going round the country visiting each store in turn, and each member will have to expect to be away from home quite a lot. Other teams are regionally organised to adapt the original designs to the specific requirements of different branches. The display team usually has its own workshop and storage areas, and may make most or all of the props, using a wide range of materials from wood to expanded polystyrene. Some members of a display team may specialise and spend all their time as studio artists, arranging windows and displays in the store. Qualities needed are a keen interest in the merchandise, colour sense and manual dexterity. Also, you need to be robust and energetic, because you have to carry around such things as stepladders, mannequins, screens and piles of merchandise, as well as furniture; the work is both creative and demanding. The minimum qualification for the job is a good general education, but sometimes up to four GCSEs, including art and English language, are required.

There are some independent display companies providing a service to shops and there are a large number of freelance display practitioners.

Opportunities for advancement, unfortunately, are limited, but with a large display staff there are opportunities for promotion to team leader, area supervisor or regional manager. Be prepared to work on Saturdays; you will get time off during the week.

Training

School-leavers interested in a career in display can train via part time or full-time BTEC, SCOTVEC, NCVA or British Display Society courses in colleges of further education. (For further details of these courses, see Chapters 9 and 10.)

Case Study

Kim aged 24, and ***Ann***, aged 18, work in a department store. They have stripped a window and have taken the stock back to the fashion departments. All that is left is a group of bald mannequins and the costume jewellery which Ann has to sort out and return to the costume jewellery buyer.

'Every item has to be accounted for and that can cause a bit of hassle. It's not only the breakages; everything in the window comes from within the store and a departmental manager will often say "You can't have this", or "Do you have to take that?" when all you're trying to do is get the dress or handbag you need for the window. The themes vary at different times of the year. Autumn is my favourite season with all the lovely rusts and browns. Of course, we're not limited just to fashion. There's the bedding window, for example, and gardening and electrical. Then we have the special festive promotions at Christmas and Easter. We're preparing the Easter theme now with a lot of colourful rabbits and eggs.'

Cashiers

Cashiers work in department stores, menswear shops, supermarkets, boutiques, TV and hi-fi stores, and fashion shops. They operate cash registers and need to know about credit accounts and cheque acceptance/credit card procedures. They may have to do a bit of selling. As the job involves handling money and meeting customers, employers tend to look for people who are responsible and trustworthy, neat, with a pleasant manner and a good standard of arithmetic. Although Saturday work is usually required, there are also compensations such as staff discounts and days off during the week.

Training

Training is carried out on the job, and larger, well-organised shops and stores will probably include off-the-job training sessions in subjects such as security and dealing with customers.

Case Study

Rita works in a menswear store. Every day, first thing, she checks the cash drawer and then looks through the order files and delivery books to see if she will have to notify customers that their suits are ready. Then there is the post to be opened. On this day, as every day, she will be totting up the takings at lunchtime – and the evenings too – so that she will know just how well the shop is doing.

'We have a credit account scheme where the customer pays a regular sum of money to me at the branch. Then we have a budget account, which involves the customer paying by standing order through a bank. This monthly printout tells me which customers are up to date with their payments and which have fallen behind. I send standard arrears letters, and hope they'll pay up.

I've always liked adding up figures. It's odd though – I have a few GCSEs but I haven't any qualifications in maths. I do a bit of training, helping the manager to show new staff how to handle cheques, cash and credit card payments and all the different paperwork. You need to be versatile.'

Computer staff

The computer field is still expanding, and computer operators, programmers and systems analysts are in great demand in the retail field.

Computer operators

A computer operator checks the temperature and humidity in the computer operations rooms, loads appropriate disks, keys instructions and keeps a record of each job.

Computer programmers

A computer programmer has to create new computer programs and amend existing ones, working together with the systems analyst who makes suggestions as to how the program should operate. The programmer looks for ambiguities, omissions and other difficulties in a program, prepares flow charts and chooses an appropriate computer language. Test runs and program modifications have to be made by the programmer.

Systems analysts

A systems analyst's job is to develop and implement new computer systems. He or she has to carry out systems investigations and decide what is required from the new system. A proposed new system has to be assessed to see if it is technically possible, and technical limitations must be explained to the users of the system. Input forms and printouts have to be designed; the system has to be broken down into procedures; a specification for the programmers has to be written; test data have to be generated to ensure that the program links logically and effectively, and the new system has to be monitored.

Educational qualifications for systems analysts will include A-level maths or Scottish Higher maths.

Laser scanning

Laser scanning is now usual in large grocery stores to control stock and to provide up-to-date information on sales trends and cash flow. A checkout operator may pass purchases through a laser beam (which reads off details of the product from a bar code consisting of black stripes), and then press a button to tot up the total. Alternatively, as in Argos stores, the customer pays for the goods required before the laser scanner calls up the goods from the warehouse to the point where the customer picks them up. Each product passed through the laser beam has its own code, which is picked up by the laser scanner. The scanner converts the code into electrical impulses which are transmitted to an in-store computer programmed to decode the signal and refer it to disk files where produce and price information are stored. The system can give an up-to-the-minute picture of sales and individual product lines, speeding up and improving reordering and stocking techniques.

Training

Some large companies, which have been using computers for a number of years, have their own training programmes for staff. Smaller companies, and companies that have had only a few years' experience with computers, tend to recruit trained staff from outside. Not all companies ask for GCSEs for trainee computer operators, although people with GCSEs and A-levels are preferred. Sometimes, computer operators progress to programming, but it is more likely that programmers will be recruited direct with A-levels or a degree.

Good computer programmers do not necessarily make good systems analysts, and the training for systems analysts is different.

Computer staff are needed in three main areas: (1) in stock control and warehousing, where automated systems have been introduced; (2) in stores which have either article numbering or checkouts linked to computers; and (3) for applying information-processing systems to the administrative sector.

Merchandisers

Merchandisers determine the range of goods sold, when to buy them, their price and how they are presented in the shop. In some companies, a merchandiser will hold a senior position with responsibility for a range of merchandise, its contents and price, and for giving policy guidelines to the buyers. In others, the merchandiser may be in a more junior management position with responsibility for merchandise promotion, which includes display units, repricing, sales forecasts and stock levels.

There is no rule of thumb about becoming a merchandiser. When advertising for a trainee or an assistant merchandiser, some companies will ask for young people with common sense, an ability with figures and a willingness to work hard. Some companies specify GCSEs and A-levels (SCE and Higher grades in Scotland) or a degree. Others recruit merchandisers from management trainees who show an aptitude in this field.

Training

The most appropriate training would be to take Levels 1 and 2 of the NVQ in Retailing, or short courses on specific topics and other BTEC, SCOTVEC or Irish NCVA qualifications (see Chapter 9).

Case Study

Rob works in a London West End store. He has to examine the merchandise to get a first-hand impression of what is selling well and what might have to be offered at a reduced price in the forthcoming sale. Some of the merchandise comes from the suppliers but most is delivered to the central warehouse where it is checked by Rob and then put into storage until required. Forecasting sales gives Rob and the buyer an idea of the quantities of merchandise they need to order.

'I'm responsible for ensuring that we always have the right level of stock in our shops. There shouldn't be too much left at the end of the season when the fashions die. Every shop is different and it is important to know what sells best in each one, so regular contact with branch managers is a good policy.

The buyer identifies trends, negotiates prices and even alters designs. Then she'll sit down with me and discuss fabrics, colours, quantities and sizes. But it's my responsibility to ensure that we don't commit all our money in high risk areas. I have to draw up our budgets so we can respond quickly to change. That may mean ploughing money into a style that's suddenly selling faster than expected. The idea is to minimise risks and maximise our profits.'

Case Study

Jim is a merchandising team leader for a supermarket group. He has a staff of three working in a huge open-plan area that doubles as an office and studio.

'Most of our work is on new or refitted stores. The retail planning department gives us the store layout, but generally it is up to us to decide on quantities of stock and the type of shelving that will be used.

We keep samples of every product we sell and put them on the shelves we are planning to use. Then, it's simply a matter of working out how many packages there are to a shelf and multiplying that by the number of shelves in a unit.

Opening day is our deadline, and as that approaches the pressure is really on. We move into the store to supervise the fitting and filling of the shelves and equipment. It's a round-the-clock operation, weekends too. Pre-planning helps to avoid problems. Timetables for deliveries and reps' visits are drawn up and the layout of the store's warehouse is worked out in advance.

When we hand over the supermarket to the manager we are handing him or her everything from the loo paper to a sales pattern and stock keeping system. Things do go wrong. Sometimes it takes longer than we expect to get a new store working properly. I once spent a month doing nights in a Manchester superstore until things were sorted out. It's a crazy life but I wouldn't like to change it.'

Buyers

Buying is based on an analysis of sales figures and new trends, so a wide knowledge of, and experience in, merchandising and selling are required. Future demands have to be forecast and large amounts of money laid out. Shops turn round their stock several times a year, and if the wrong stock is bought financial resources are wasted. Over-buying or bad judgement means surplus stock, and under-buying may mean loss of customers because items are out of stock and customers go elsewhere. Accurate forecasts have to be made for the months or year ahead, depending on the goods being sold.

In large organisations, millions of pounds' worth of stock will be bought. Sales figures are studied to find out how much customers have been spending and the type of goods to which they are attracted. The buyer has to decide what customers want, determine the range and level of stock, find suppliers, select merchandise, negotiate the best price and terms, and decide when and how much to buy. He or she has to be flexible to allow for the change in customers' tastes and the amount of the given product they buy. The aim is to obtain goods and services 'of the right quality, in the right quantity, from the right source, delivered to the right place at the right time, at the right price'.

In small companies only one person is responsible for all these tasks; in larger firms people specialise in particular aspects, and there may be a team of several dozen buyers at head office buying for all the firm's branches.

Buyers are usually recruited from successful sales and management staff, so the first step should be to join a firm as a management trainee or as a member of the sales staff. Occasionally, firms advertise for trainee buyers, but it is very unlikely that anyone would be taken on as a buyer straight from school.

The minimum qualifications needed to become a buyer are four GCSEs, including English language and maths, and one A-level, or, in Scotland, five SCE subjects, including three at Higher grade, and Ordinary grade English.

Training

Most of the larger companies have developed their own internal training programmes, supplemented by short courses on buying topics. The Institute of Purchasing and Supply (see page 78) runs courses which are widely recognised and relevant to the work of all buyers. (See Chapter 9 for details of these courses.)

Case Study

Simon *is an assistant furniture buyer with a co-operative society. One of his many duties is ensuring that goods are delivered to the shops at the right time and in the correct quantity. He spends a lot of time on the telephone dealing with suppliers, advertising people and the society's many branches that spread from Nottingham to Skegness, some 90 miles away.*

'Popping over there for a few minutes isn't exactly a practical proposition. There's the paperwork side of the business – helping my boss, the buyer, to forecast demand and control the amount of furniture kept at each branch – and there is the opportunity to get out to furniture exhibitions and to manufacturers' previews when they launch a new range.'

Case Study

Liz *is a group outerwear buyer.*

'I started my career with a degree in zoology and physiology. Outerwear was my third buyership – and then I started adding stores! Buying is the part of retailing I enjoy most, so I have developed my career along that line.

I get a kick out of making the best profit I can. I'm always competing with myself to beat last season's figures. I put each range together in my mind first, making sure it's balanced to suit the customers. The customer profile differs in each store – styles, size scales and preferred colours vary around the country – which gives an added dimension to the task!

I'm away, on average, for three or four days in every fortnight, attending shows and visiting manufacturers' showrooms. I often negotiate on price, so building up a good relationship is very important. When I'm in the store I catch up on my orders and admin work, as well as getting out on the sales floor. I rely on my underbuyer for the day-to-day running of the department, and to keep up the team spirit.

Knowing what will sell is very instinctive, and I have to be prepared to commit myself and take risks. I thrive on the pressure – no two days are the same and I'm always so busy that it's a kind of permanent 'high'. You have to put your whole self into this job – there are no half measures – I love it.'

Retail managers

The duties of retail managers vary considerably according to the type and size of the firm. Modern retail management is a very complex activity, requiring managers with the ability to understand and apply modern management techniques and to develop and control large-scale retail outlets. It is important to remember that each company has different duties for each manager and the following job descriptions are intended to be only a general guide to the retail management field.

Retail organisations recruit managers from a number of sources, including those who are experienced junior staff, holders of A-levels or Highers, and graduates.

Management training schemes often include on-the-job training, combined with short, intensive courses on certain aspects of retailing. Levels 3 and 4 of the NVQ in Retailing have been designed to help train retail managers.

Branch manager

The branch manager organises and controls all branch activities and is involved in the day-to-day running of the branch as laid down by head office. The pay is good, but the hours are long. Duties vary according to the size and type of firm, but most branch managers are responsible for recruiting and selecting staff and arranging for their training. They also control display and window dressing, and have to monitor the general condition and maintenance of the premises, including hygiene. Branch managers are also responsible for stock levels, sales promotion and service to the customers. They should always be striving to increase sales with a high standard of sales skills, attending to customers and dealing with their complaints, and making sure that the merchandise is presented in an attractive way.

The branch manager needs to keep in touch with local trends and conditions, ensuring that local advertising is effective so that all opportunities to increase sales may be taken and the relevant information fed back to head office. The branch manager is also responsible for security and should, for example, check that the branch is locked at the end of the day, that fire precautions are adequate, and that there are minimal unaccounted stock losses. The daily cash balance has to be checked every night, and the cash has to be taken to and from the bank.

In large stores, the branch manager is responsible to head office and directly responsible to the area or regional manager.

There are opportunities to progress to area or regional manager, to buyer or floor controller, or to a senior position at head office.

Case Study

Philip is manager of a two-floor shoe shop. He is in the shop every morning before anyone else, checking the till at 8.00 am. At opening time everything is spick and span and his two full-time assistants and four cadet managers are ready for another day's trading.

'Unless I have a specific job to do I normally spend most of the day on the shop floor, serving customers, making sure everyone gets a break at the proper time, and generally seeing that everything runs smoothly.

I am responsible for the staff, the security of the shop and everything in it. It's my job to make sure that we sell all we possibly can, while keeping the running costs of the place to a minimum. What I don't like is losing staff, especially if I have to terminate their employment. Among other things it means I was wrong about them, although I'm learning from my mistakes.'

Departmental manager

A departmental manager may be found in multiple grocery stores (for example, a greengrocery manager) or in chain stores (for example, a ladies' fashion department manager), but usually a departmental manager is a manager in a department store. The position may carry more responsibility than that of a branch manager and is usually a more senior appointment. It is likely that a departmental manager will be responsible for buying as well as selling, and will be responsible for a greater number of staff, organising where they work and dealing with general personnel problems. Like the branch manager, the departmental manager is responsible for meeting sales targets, sales promotion, security and relations with customers.

The departmental manager may aim for promotion to sales floor controller, responsible for a number of departments, or to another senior administrative post, perhaps at head office.

Case Study

Kevin is manager of the men's outfitting department of a Kingston department store. His career began when he joined the store at the age of 16. He had GCSEs and so was accepted for the trainee management scheme. He was moved from department to department to gain experience.

'I suppose I wouldn't have gone into retailing if I didn't enjoy meeting people and feeling good every time a customer decides to buy.

The success of the department depends to some extent on knowing what the customers want and then influencing the buyer to get the right clothing in the right quality, quantity, colour and range of sizes. Success also depends on an ability to keep overheads to a minimum, which means tight security, careful checks on all deliveries and invoices, and keeping accurate records of the movement of goods in and out of the department.

The quality of my team is obviously very important to me. In addition to recommending individuals for courses which I think will help their development, I follow the progress of my management trainees and encourage training on the sales floor when trade is slack.

I have had to understudy a lot of managers in my five years in the business, and I've been taught a lot, too.'

Supermarket manager

The supermarket manager is the head of a supermarket superstore or hypermarket, and is responsible for the store. He or she will have to be fit, hard-working and practical and ready for many intellectual challenges as the job is very demanding. It is necessary to be able to thrive on pressure, think on your feet and be able to remember one thing while listening to another! Quick decision making is also necessary.

As store managers are responsible for both people and products, they should enjoy meeting people and take a pride in the products they sell. They have to put the customer first, notice the customer who needs help, and put up with the customer who doesn't but who is determined to moan!

A store manager has to consider the staff at all times and help them to understand their jobs, which means that he or she has to know the jobs of the other staff better than they do, and be able to help out if necessary. You cannot expect others to do what you would not do yourself.

The job requires foresight and planning, and you need to be numerate and logical. The planning of a store involves intensive work liaising with the head office of the company and considering the needs of the store weeks in advance. Another need is to know how the law impinges on retailing, for example, weights and measures, health and safety at work, food and drugs, the Trade Descriptions Act, and staff employment regulations.

Most important of all, a supermarket manager has to know how each department is doing and whether or not the targets are being met. Products move fast in a supermarket, so it may mean a daily ordering of many lines.

Managers should be well trained and well educated, perhaps up to degree standard.

Training

Most supermarket groups now have trainee management schemes for which they recruit people with A-levels or a business studies qualification, as well as graduates.

You will be given courses introducing you to the various

departments of a supermarket. You will learn the techniques of ordering and display, how to sell and how to supervise the staff. After about six months as an initial graduate trainee you will become an assistant department manager. Then, after further training, you will become a department manager and finally a supermarket manager.

Case Study

Sara and *Bill* talk about their lives as supermarket managers.

'A good day is when you have a whole lot of problems facing you first thing – for instance, someone hasn't come in, someone else is on holiday or ill, two freezers have broken down, and the electricians are coming to install a new display – and, by the end of the day, you have sorted your way through all the difficulties.

When the shop is very full and the shelves are emptying fast, you have to make quick decisions about deploying staff. You can't hang around for 10 minutes wondering what to do next. And you mustn't let your staff see you falter or hesitate – you must give them immediate answers.

You need to organise your day to get things in the right order: worry and solve major problems – don't get bogged down with minor ones. You must sort out your priorities.

Sometimes at the end of a bank holiday week when you've been working 12 or 14 hours at a stretch, you think about your friends who work from 9.00 am to 5.00 pm. But then you realise that you wouldn't be happy doing their sort of job. The hours in this work may be long, but the money is good.

If you are open with your staff they will bring you their problems, which often affect how they are working. You find out what areas they like best, try to move them around and encourage them to look beyond what they think are their immediate abilities.

Most customers simply want help, and some are almost embarrassingly grateful. A few seem to come here to complain, and all you can do is stand there and take what they say while they get it out of their systems. They don't really want explanations.'

Personnel manager

The personnel manager recruits, trains and organises staff, administers salaries and catering facilities, and looks after health and welfare. The work includes the planning of staff needs and devising work schedules. In large stores personnel managers may spend a lot of time on the shop floor reallocating staff to cope with gaps or fluctuations in sales. The job will appeal to people who like dealing with other people – understanding them, recruiting them, training them, and safeguarding their conditions and welfare. The personnel manager must remain approachable and be able to act as a counsellor when needed. He or she also needs to be able to lead and organise other people.

In large firms, as they are the functional head of the personnel department, personnel managers have director status, but in smaller firms they would be under the store manager's supervision.

A large number of people in personnel work start their careers on the sales side or as trainee staff managers. You will become an assistant personnel manager after about six months and then, after some years' service, the personnel manager. In large firms you could move on to the position of area personnel manager, or to a personnel position at head office.

You may need a degree on entry. Minimum qualifications are five GCSEs, including two at A-level, or, in Scotland, five SCE subjects, including three Highers and O-grade English.

Training

Many firms require personnel staff to take the Institute of Personnel Development (IPD) courses (see Chapter 9 for details). Training in the store will last up to two years and will normally consist of in-store and external training schemes with the emphasis on attaining staff management skills.

Case Study

Jackie is 18 and an assistant personnel manager who helps to look after the welfare and training of some 90 Saturday staff and over 100 full- and part-time employees in a company store. She has completed a junior management training scheme.

'I thought my age would be a problem. Luckily it seems to give a rapport with the women who tend to come to me with their problems instead of going to a department manager. The older staff are very friendly too.

I suppose I could have specialised in a job behind the scenes but I am interested in the people and the personnel management side of the store.

The training has obviously boosted my self-confidence. I mean, I couldn't give a half-hour training session every Wednesday morning had I not been sent on a course that dealt with training and instructing people.

There is the attraction of dealing with the unexpected. One minute I might be sorting out a problem for one of the women; the next I might be dealing with a telephone call from the DSS. I have also had to put my knowledge of first aid to use in one or two minor accidents.'

Conclusion

There are many other jobs in the retailing world, but those which have been described above are some of the most important. Throughout the following chapters you will find that they appear again and, again, sometimes under different names. Always remember, however, that no two firms have exactly the same job categories, so that, for example, a branch manager's role in one firm will not be quite the same as in another. You will also find many jobs that have not been mentioned in this chapter, some of which are very specialised.

5 Allied professions: a brief outline

There are two industries closely allied to retailing, both of which are in the distribution sector, as described on page 5.

Marketing

There are lots of degrees in marketing, all of which are listed in the *UCAS Handbook*. If you are interested, phone the relevant universities listed for brochures about the courses provided.

The Institute of Sales and Marketing Management provides two distance learning programmes related to marketing: a 75-hour study course on professional salesmanship and a sales management course designed to cover the roles of management in depth. The latter course is designed to take about 150 hours altogether.

The Chartered Institute of Marketing, Europe's largest professional body for marketing and sales practitioners, provides a large variety of courses at both junior level and degree level, with the International Diploma in Marketing.

Warehousing

This industry has recently become increasingly important as each year there is a significant increase in the variety of goods and number of each variety stored in bulk. This is in part because of the additional opening hours and also owing to the growing number of people who order their groceries over the phone or on the Internet. In any event, warehouse workers are currently much in demand. They use computers to order and check their stock. Many stores have storage depots that supply shops as and when necessary. These require operators who drive fork lift trucks, assemble orders, or drive trailers. This is skilled work that can only be undertaken by those aged 18+ with appropriate licences.

NVQs in Warehousing are available from City & Guilds at Levels 1–4. Units include: Dealing with customers, Controlling and maintaining stock, Assembling orders and Co-ordinating and controlling sales and marketing. For further information, see Chapter 2 of this book, pages 4–8.

6 Getting started and finding a job

Getting started

So, you've decided you're going for a job in retailing. Having made the decision, what do you do next?

Before you do anything else, think hard about your decision. Have you *really* decided to go for it? A golden rule to remember is that you have to really want to do something before you can do it. A half-baked attempt to find a job will lead nowhere. But if you are determined, absolutely sure you want the job and are focused on what you are doing, you can't go wrong.

Once you are sure you want to go ahead, you can set about finding a job.

Finding a job

How do you find a job in retailing? There are a number of different ways of doing this. Many large companies advertise vacancies in national and local newspapers or on television. Or you could go to the careers service and find out if there is anything available.

You might want to apply direct to a shop to see if there are any vacancies, and in fact many stores encourage this method of application. You could just walk into a shop on a quiet day (say, Monday or Tuesday) and ask to speak to the manager, who will give you the information you require about vacancies, hours of work, salaries and benefits, etc. If there is a definite vacancy, the manager may say whether he or she considers the job suitable for you and may help you to decide whether you definitely want to apply for it.

If you find the idea of walking into a shop a bit daunting, you could always write a letter or telephone. If you phone, ask for an application form for the job, or, if one is not available, ask for an interview. Come straight to the point, and say something like: 'I'm ringing about the job advertised in today's paper/on the television/in the window. It sounds very interesting. Could you tell me more about it, please?' If you are writing a letter, ask whether there are vacancies of the type you require (if you don't know already) and for further information and an application form. On a *separate sheet of paper*, give some *brief* details about your age, where you were educated and your qualifications. This is called your curriculum vitae (see below).

You may have a friend or relative who knows of a job available in your area and can help you. Perhaps he or she already works in the store you want to work in, in which case you can learn about the people you might be going to work with, what sort of money you are likely to earn, what the building is like, and the way the staff are treated. All these things are very important and will determine whether you are going to be happy or unhappy in a job.

Listen to what your friend or relative has to say. If it sounds attractive, then you can apply feeling confident that at least one person likes working for the shop you are considering. If, on the other hand, the prospects sound gloomy, you can decide either to forget the whole thing, or apply anyway, on the basis that there might be a good job for you, even though the person giving you the information is unhappy. And it just might be that you know he or she is liable to moan about most things – so ignore the gloomy side, pick out the good bits, and decide, if you are asked to attend an interview, to judge for yourself.

Help for people with disabilities

Disability Employment Advisers advise about special needs, difficulties such as obtaining work, or health problems, and can help you to find a job.

More information can be obtained from the Department of Employment, Moorfoot, Sheffield S1 4PQ; 0114 275 3275.

The letter of application and application form

If you are phoning the shop you want to work in, you may well be asked to attend an interview immediately, or possibly have an interview over the telephone. If, however, you are applying for a job through the post you will have to write a letter of application for the job. You should be very careful about this letter. *Keep it short and to the point.* The person receiving it will not want a torn or dirty bit of paper, full of words that are difficult to read because they are misspelt, or a letter written in scrawly writing. It is best to check your spelling first in a draft letter, and then type it, if possible. Mention where you saw the advertisement for the vacancy you are applying for (if there is a definite vacancy), and keep a copy of the letter for reference.

After you have sent an initial letter you may receive an application form. Application forms are carefully designed and ask for personal details about your education, job experience, and other activities and interests. You should fill in the form, answering all the questions asked, and keep your answers as short as possible unless asked to do otherwise.

The curriculum vitae

You may be asked to send in a curriculum vitae (CV), if you haven't already done so. This is a summary of your life to date, with details of your educational background, qualifications and work experience. A CV should be typed, if possible, and should not be more that two pages long. It should give the following details:

◆ Full name and address
◆ Date of birth
◆ Schools attended

◆ Examinations passed
◆ Any other honours won at school
◆ Any position of authority held at school (eg school captain)
◆ Training courses or colleges attended and qualifications gained
◆ Previous jobs held, if any
◆ Present employment, if any
◆ Details of any work experience such as holiday or Saturday jobs
◆ Personal interests or hobbies (if you have a current driving licence, mention it here)
◆ Names and addresses of two referees (one of these should be a previous employer or someone who has some knowledge of your capabilities).

The interview

You will almost certainly be asked for an interview before starting a new job. You may feel nervous about this – almost everyone does, no matter how many interviews they have been through. You will find interviews less frightening if you remember that all interviews have a structure.

The interviewer will start by trying to put you at your ease, making small talk about the weather, trains or buses. The talk will turn fairly swiftly to your career to date, and you will be asked what you have done since you left school, etc. The interviewer wants you to talk so that he or she can gain an impression of what you are like. Don't blather, but at the same time don't give 'yes' or 'no' answers to every question. Say why you want the job and how you think you would fit in, and what your career ambitions are. You will probably be asked if you have a clear picture of the job and what it entails. This is to see if you have given some thought to it.

At the end of the interview you will probably be asked if you have any questions, and you must try to think of something to ask. If it looks as though you are going to be offered the job, this is the time to clear up anything you are not sure about. You should ask about how much money you will receive a week; how your training will be organised; how many weeks' holidays you are entitled to, etc. The interviewer will be pleased you have asked these questions, as it will be obvious you are showing real interest in the job and that you are well motivated. Finally you should ask to see round the store, so that you can have a good look at the place where you might be working, and perhaps meet some of the people you might be working with.

Accepting a job

Before you receive your contract of employment and write your official letter of acceptance, you should make sure you know exactly where you stand. You should know the sort of things you are going to be expected to do in the job, what your hours and rates of pay are, and how many weeks' holidays you get a year. You should make sure you know all these things *before* you accept the job offer – preferably at the interview (see above). It is no use saying that you didn't realise what the job involved, or that you thought you were entitled to five weeks' holiday and it turns out to be only three, after you have accepted the job and are already working in the firm.

Contract of employment

A contract of employment exists as soon as someone offers you a job, even verbally, at a certain rate of pay, and you accept. Within two months of your starting work, whether full time or part time, the employer is required by law to give you written particulars of certain key terms of your contract. These cover the following:

◆ Names of employer and employee
◆ Date when employment (and continuous employment) began
◆ Expected period of employment or date of termination if

      employment is temporary or for a fixed term
♦ Job title and job description
♦ Place of work, or whether you are required to work in various locations
♦ Pay
♦ Sickness or injury and sick pay
♦ How you are paid (weekly, monthly, etc)
♦ Hours of work
♦ Holiday entitlement and pay
♦ Length of notice
♦ Disciplinary and grievance procedures
♦ Pension rights
♦ Collective agreements.

If you are not given these particulars within two months of joining a company, you should ask for them. All documents that you receive from your employer are important, and may comprise part of your contract of employment, so make sure you keep them in a safe place.

Your contract may be subject to your employer receiving satisfactory references. You may also be placed on an initial probationary period for the first few months to assess your suitability. During such a period you may not enjoy the same level of benefits as your colleagues in permanent positions; for example, leave may be at the discretion of your manager. If your employer is not fully satisfied with your performance he or she may dismiss you during or at the end of your probationary period or may extend the period of probation.

Dress and appearance

You may be expected to wear a uniform and/or conform to an appropriate standard of dress or appearance. You might also be required to wear protective clothing for health and safety reasons. If, however, you are from an ethnic background which imposes strict dress or appearance codes, your employer should not discriminate against you by imposing requirements which conflict with these codes.

Part-time working

Part-time workers now have the same employment protection rights as full-time workers, regardless of the number of hours they work per week. For example, both part-time and full-time workers have the right not to be unfairly dismissed and the right to a redundancy payment provided they have worked for the same employer for at least two years. Also, part-time staff who are women are, like their full-time female colleagues, protected from detrimental treatment which amounts to sex discrimination.

Sunday trading

A change in the law in 1994 permitted all retailers to open on Sundays. Large stores can open for six continuous hours between 10 am and 6 pm. However, shopworkers who do not want to work on Sundays for whatever reason are protected against unfair dismissal or any other detrimental treatment if they exercise their right not to work on Sundays, unless they are employed to work only on Sundays.

If you are not required to work on Sundays and cannot be required to do so under your contract of employment, even if the new rights on Sunday working are disregarded, you are protected from Sunday working. If, however, your job began after 25 August 1994 and you are, or may be, required to work on Sundays you should be given a notice by your employer informing you of your right to 'opt out' of Sunday working. If you do object, you will need to give your employer a written notice saying that you object to working on Sundays. This notice will not take effect until three months after you give it. If, subsequently, you undertake work on a Sunday, you will lose your right to opt out, and must repeat the notice procedure. Note, however, that you cannot object to Sunday working if you are employed to work only on Sundays.

Deductions from pay

There are special provisions for deductions from pay for cash shortages or stock deficiencies for employees in retailing. A deduction can only be made if it is required or authorised by law or by a provision in your contract of employment, or if you have previously given your written and signed consent to it.

Your employer is entitled to make deductions from your salary for cash shortages or stock deficiencies of up to 10 per cent of your gross pay on any given pay day, except for your last pay packet in which case the 10 per cent restriction will not apply to any deductions made. Your employer is allowed to recoup the shortage or deficiency over a number of salary payments, but the deduction can only be made, or a series of deductions commenced, within 12 months of the discovery of the shortage or deficiency.

Flexible working patterns

There is a growing trend in the retailing sector for flexible working patterns. This means that you can be employed to work a certain number of hours per week, but that, when you work, those hours will vary from week to week. Employers in such circumstances require flexibility from their employees and you should find out before you accept a new job what hours you will be expected to work to ensure that you can fulfil the employer's requirements or that you will be guaranteed a minimum number of working hours.

The degree of flexibility available to employers in fixing working patterns will be restricted once the European Working Time Directive is implemented in the UK. The Directive includes provisions to impose an average maximum working week of 48 hours, minimum requirements for annual holidays and daily and weekly rest periods and special provisions for night workers. However, until the Directive is implemented by the UK government, its impact on employment practice in the UK retail sector will remain uncertain. (The Directive is likely to be implemented at the end of 1997).

Equal opportunities

Your employer should have implemented an equal opportunities policy to ensure the recruitment process and workplace are free from discrimination on the grounds of sex, race or disability.

Sex or racial discrimination may occur either where a person is treated less favourably because of his or her sex or race (direct discrimination), or where an employer imposes an unjustifiable condition which you are unable to satisfy because of your sex or race (indirect discrimination).

Disability discrimination occurs where a person is unjustifiably disadvantaged because of a disability. Your employer may be required to make reasonable adjustments to the workplace or recruitment process to prevent discrimination. For these purposes a disability is a physical or mental impairment which has a substantial and long-term adverse affect on a person's ability to carry out normal day-to-day activities.

7 Getting in and getting on

for Getting into Retailing

◆ *Keep an eye on the local and national newspapers.* All sorts of jobs – from part-time sales assistant to trainee management positions – are advertised in the press.

◆ *Take a voluntary job or part-time work* for a short time before you apply for a 'proper' job in retailing. That way you can find out if you like the work and, if you do, you will be able to say that you've had some valuable work experience later, when you go for an interview. You will show you are both willing and keen to work, and you will have gained useful experience of dealing with customers. In any situation, you will be learning on the job, both how to do it right and, most important, how not to make mistakes!

◆ *Keep abreast of current trends.* Whatever sector of retailing you are interested in, there will be factors that affect sales, the product and the methods of retailing. Read up on your chosen topic, whether it be fashion magazines or the building trade press. Any knowledge you acquire will help to make you a better informed, more useful member of the organisation you wish to enter.

◆ *Don't be late.* Timekeeping is very important. Shops open at set hours, and you can't afford to turn up late and find a group of irate customers banging on the closed doors.

Remember, other people depend on you doing your job properly, so don't let them down. And when you go for an interview it is, of course, essential that you turn up at the time agreed.

◆ *Look neat.* You are unlikely to be taken on anywhere if your hair is unkempt and straggly, or your clothes look ruffled and ragged. In most retailing positions you are on display, and so you must look the part.

◆ *Look alert, look interested – and try to smile.* No one is going to bother with you if you appear listless, bored and grumpy. Remember, *retailing is all about people.* You have to show you want to be with others. A pleasing face with a smile shows a likeable person who will probably fit in. You won't be the only pebble on the beach – in most cases there will be many people working with you.

8 The future of retailing

Over the next five years or so, there is going to be a far greater demand for certain jobs. For example, because people are finding it more difficult to go shopping during the time when shops are normally open, a few (currently, in 1997, not that many) retailers have already made it much easier for customers to order their goods by phone, and an increasing number of people are using the Internet to place orders for their bulk shopping. This means there will be a greater demand for people to deliver goods from shop or, more likely, warehouse to home and for packers to pack up the boxes.

At the same time, and again because of the difficulty a lot of people find in shopping during 'normal' working hours, there will be an increasing number of shops open for 24 hours every day, except Sundays. There will be a demand for people prepared to work unsocial hours, and since 1994 with the change in trading hours there has already been a noticeable increase in shift work in retailing. This might suit a couple with children, with one partner working while the other minds the children, alternating the work and child care over a 24-hour period. Such a pattern of work, however, although perhaps satisfactory financially, is likely to cause stress.

Ever more shops in cities and large towns are opening on Sundays following the 1994 Sunday Opening Act (see page 62). This again will mean more jobs available for people who might need the work during times when most people don't work. At the same time, working on Sunday is likely to markedly affect people's lives outside their work: their social life, their lives with their families, etc.

The numbers of supermarkets, hypermarkets and shopping centres (lots of stores together under one roof) are likely to increase somewhat. Space, however, is very limited, particularly in the populated areas of southern England and the Midlands. Stringent planning regulations and environmental concerns will ensure the numbers will be limited.

Both government and local authorities are anxious to encourage the regeneration of inner city retailing, and there is evidence that some positive forward planning is proving fruitful. There is a major problem, however, regarding traffic, with congestion and pollution, both of which tend to limit the number of customers shopping. There does nevertheless appear to be a slight increase in the number of stores opening in large urban areas.

A change of government in May 1997 means that within five years the UK will almost certainly have a minimum wage agreement. This will benefit people working in retailing, particularly those working as sales assistants, many of whom have for a very long time been paid very low wages.

9 Qualifications available

Degree courses

Institutions offering degree courses in retailing are listed in Chapter 10. The courses are usually either three years full-time or four years sandwich. Applications for degrees in England, Wales, Scotland and Northern Ireland should be made through the Universities and Colleges Admissions Service (UCAS), or in the Republic of Ireland through the Universities Central Application office in Galway. Look at the *UCAS Handbook* which provides details of admission procedures and how to apply. Applications are normally made between 1 September and 15 December of the year preceding the year of entry.

While tuition fees for almost all first degree courses are likely to be paid automatically, you will still have to find ways of financing living expenses. Maintenance grants may be awarded. The maximum maintenance grant (1997) for students living away from home and staying outside London is £1,700. For students in London away from home it is £2,105 and for students living at home in London £1,400. This maximum is reduced on a sliding scale according to parents' income. As a student you will need at least £5,000 per year to cover accommodation, books, travel, clothes and other living costs.

Other general qualifications in retailing

Very brief guides to important qualifications are listed below. For information about institutions providing the courses or awarding bodies, see Chapter 10.

BTEC Higher National Diploma in Distribution Studies

For those who wish to work or who are already working at a senior level in the retail industry. It is equivalent to a pass degree of NVQ Level 4 and is available only at the University of Ulster.

BTEC One-year Intermediate Retail and Distributive Services Award

Equivalent to NVQ Level 2. Students should be aged 16+.

BTEC Advanced Retail and Distributive Services in Distribution

Equivalent to two A-levels or NVQ Level 3. Students should be aged 16+.

General National Vocational Qualifications (GNVQs) in Retail and Distributive Services

These qualifications provide students with a broad view of the different operations of retailing and distribution. Units include: Investigating distribution operations, Types of transport and supply chain for retail products, Investigating the retail sector, Carrying out a market research survey, Producing a transport plan.

National Vocational Qualifications (NVQs) in Retailing

These are offered at Levels 1–4. Units available include: Retail sales delivery, Retail operations, Distributive operations, Displaying and merchandising stock, Customer service and staff development.

General Scottish Vocational Qualifications (GSVQs)

These are designed for 16- to 19-year-olds in schools and also for adult returners. They help with a broad range of employment such as business administration and are available at three levels: Foundation, Intermediate and Advanced.

Scottish Vocational Qualifications (SVQs)

These are made up of National Certificate modules, Higher National units or Workplace Assessed units and can be built up over time. They include SVQs in Retailing, Levels 1–5.

National Council Vocational Awards (NCVAs)

These are available in the Republic of Ireland at Foundation, Level 1 and Level 2. Some are specifically relevant to retailing.

Specialist courses

Details are provided of some but by no means all of the very wide range of specialist courses in retailing.

Bookselling

UK and Irish Diploma in Bookselling
Modules include: Customers and service, Methods of payment, Stock care and management, Bibliography and Consumer and retail law for bookshops.

Buying

Fundamentals of Purchasing and Supply
A number of programmes designed for people who are either new to the purchasing function or who have had little formal training.

Graduate Diploma in Purchasing and Supply
Modules include: Purchasing, Marketing, Operations management, Business accounting, Commercial relations, Retail merchandise management and International purchasing.

There are many short courses in purchasing and an NVQ Level
4 in Procurement.

Clocks and watches

There is a correspondence course in technical horology available
on both the theoretical and practical aspects, divided into three
grades: Preliminary, Intermediate and Final.

Display

BDS Technician Certificate
A part-time three-year course for students aged 16+.

BDS National Diploma (Advanced Level) in Retail Display
A two-year full-time course for students aged 16+.

BDS National Diploma (Advanced Level) in Exhibition Design
A full-time two-year course.

BDS Point of Sale Certificate

Grocery

Foundation Certificate in Management
Provides junior managers with a structured introduction to the
food industry.

Postgraduate Certificate in Food and Grocery Industry
Management
Provides a flexible vehicle to develop the knowledge, skills and
understanding of middle managers in the food and grocery industry.

Certificate in Food and Grocery Industry Management
A postgraduate programme to provide a flexible framework to develop the knowledge, skills and understanding of middle managers within the food and grocery industry.

A large number of short courses are also available.

Health

RSA certificates and diplomas are available in the following subjects: Health and safety management, Food and health, Essential food hygiene, Food hygiene awareness, Food hygiene management, Nutrition for food and catering management, Meat inspection, Inspection of meat and other foods, Environmental protection, Pest control, Basic oral health promotion, Health and hygiene for hairdressers, Counselling in health care, Asbestos management.

Jewellery

Diploma in Gemmology
This is concerned with the study of gemstones and deals with the occurrence, physical properties and identification of natural, synthetic and imitation gemstones.

Gem Diamond Diploma
An internationally recognised qualification enabling you to identify and assess diamonds to a recognised standard of excellence.

Retail Jeweller's Diploma
The NVQ training award for the retail jewellery trade. There is a one-year preliminary course followed by a one-year diploma course.

Retail Gemstone Course
This follows on from the Diploma and is designed to provide comprehensive knowledge of all major varieties of gemstones encountered in the trade.

Personnel

There are many short courses available including the following: Essential interviewing skills, Counselling in the workplace, Managing stress, Job evaluation, Employee benefits and pensions, Training evaluation and assessment, Complete employment law, Leadership for the new millennium, Navigating change, Effective presentation skills, Positive influencing skills, Essential interpersonal skills, Feedback and counselling skills for trainers, Introduction to psychology for trainers and Training design.

Pharmacy

There are 16 schools of pharmacy providing four-year pharmacy degree courses in four broad subject areas: the origin and chemistry of drugs (medical chemistry); the preparation of medicines (pharmaceutics); the action and uses of drugs and medicines (pharmacology), and pharmacy practice (the social, legal and ethical aspects of pharmacy). All pharmacy graduates intending to register as pharmacists to practise their profession have to complete an approved degree course together with an extra one-year period of practical pre-registration training in a pharmaceutical establishment.

Stationery and office equipment

Diploma in Office Systems and Stationery
This covers subjects such as health and safety, customer care, telephone techniques, merchandising, paper and board, envelopes and bags, computer data, processing equipment. There is also a wide range of distance learning courses available.

Wines and spirits

Certificate
For people with little or no experience of handling wines, spirits and other alcoholic beverages.

Higher Certificate

For those occupying supervisory positions in the wine trade.

Diploma

For those requiring a detailed contemporary knowledge of the production and commercial significance of wines and spirits in the UK.

10 Where to study

Colleges and universities

University of Abertay Dundee, Information and Recruitment Office, Bell Street, Dundee DD1 1HG; 01382 308000

Birmingham College of Food, Tourism and Creative Studies, Undergraduate Admissions Office, Summer Row, Birmingham B3 1JB; 0121 604 1000

Bournemouth University, The Registrar, Talbot Campus, Fern Barrow, Poole, Dorset BH12 5BB; 01202 524111

University of Brighton, Admissions, Academic Registry, Mithras House, Lewes Road, Brighton BN2 4AT; 01273 600900

Glasgow Caledonian University, Admissions Office, City Campus, 70 Cowcaddens Road, Glasgow G4 0BA; 0141 331 3000

University of Greenwich, Course Enquiries Officer, Wellington Street, Woolwich, London SE18 6PF; 0800 005 006

University of Huddersfield, Marketing, Retailing and Distribution, Schools and Colleges Liaison Officer, Queensgate, Huddersfield, West Yorkshire HD1 3HD; 01484 422288

London College of Printing and Distributive Trades, School of Retail Studies, 65 Davies Street, London W1Y 2DA; 0171 514 6500

London Institute, Communications and Marketing Department, 65 Davies Street, London W1Y 2DA; 0171 514 6000

Loughborough University, Senior Assistant Registrar, Admissions Office, Ashby Road, Loughborough, Leicestershire LE11 3TU; 01509 263171

Manchester Metropolitan University, Applications Section, Academic Division, All Saints, Manchester M15 6BH; 0161 247 1035

University of North London, Course Enquiries Office, Holloway Road, London N7 8DB; 0171 753 5066

Queen Margaret College, Admissions Officer, Clerwood Terrace, Edinburgh EH12 8TS; 0131 317 3440

Roehampton Institute, Admissions Officer, Roehampton Lane, London SW15 5PU; 0181 392 3000

University of Stirling, The Course Administrator, The Distance Learning Portfolio, Institute for Retail Studies, University of Stirling, Stirling, FK9 4LA; 01786 467044

University of Surrey, Undergraduate Admissions Officer, Guildford, Surrey GU2 5XH; 01483 259305

University of Ulster, Admissions Officer, Cromore Road, Coleraine, County Londonderry BT52 1SA; 01265 44141

Other main institutions

British Display Society, 70a Crayford High Street, Dartford, Kent DA1 4EF; 01322 550544 (display workers)

British Shops and Stores Association, Middleton House, 2 Main Road, Middleton Cheney, Banbury, Oxfordshire OX17 2TN; 01295 712277 (independent and specialist retailers)

Business and Technology Education Council (BTEC), c/o Edexcel Foundation, Stewart House, 32 Russell Square, London WC1B 5DN; 0171 393 4444 (awarding body for BTEC qualifications)

Chartered Institue of Marketing, Moor Hall, Cookham, Maidenhead, Berkshire SL6 9QH; 01628 427500

City & Guilds of London Institute, 1 Giltspur Street, London EC1A 9DD; 0171 294 3167 (awarding body for NVQs/GNVQs)

Distributive OSC, The CODA Centre, 189 Munster Road, London SW6 6AW; 0171 386 5599 (development of NVQs/GNVQs in the distributive sector)

Dublin Institute of Technology, School of Retail and Service Management, Fitzwilliam House, 30 Upper Pembroke Street, Dublin 2; 01 402 3000 (for information about a future degree course (1998) in retailing, and further studies)

Institute of Grocery Distribution, Grange Lane, Letchmore Heath, Watford WD2 8DQ; 01923 857141 (grocery sector)

Institute of Personnel Development, IPD House, 35 Camp Road, Wimbledon, London SW19 4UX; 0181 971 9000 (personnel)

Institute of Purchasing and Supply, Easton House, Church Street, Easton on the Hill, Stamford, Lincolnshire PE9 3NZ; 01780 756777 (buyers)

Institute of Sales and Marketing Management, The College of Sales and Marketing, PO Box 49, Luton, Bedfordshire LU1 2RD; 01582 411130

Meat Training Council, PO Box 141, Winterhill House, Snowdon Drive, Milton Keynes MK6 1YY; 01908 231062 (grocery sector)

National Vocational Qualifications Association Ireland, National Council for Vocational Awards, Marino Institute of Education, Griffith House, Dublin 9; 01 837 2211 (Irish association for NCVA awards)

Retail Training Consultancy Council, 1 Glenville Terrace, Dublin 14; 01 298 2722 (for information about retailing institutions and training in the Republic of Ireland)

Royal Pharmaceutical Society of Great Britain, 1 Lambeth High Street, London SE1 7JN; 0171 735 9141 (pharmacy)

Royal Society of Health, RSH House, 38a St George's Drive, London SW1V 4BA; 0171 630 0121 (health)

Scottish Vocational Education Council (SCOTVEC), Hanover House, 24 Douglas Street, Glasgow G2 7NQ; 0141 248 7900 (SVQ awarding body)

Specialist institutions

Booksellers' Association of Great Britain and Ireland, Booksellers' Association Training Department, 272 Vauxhall Bridge Road, London SW1V 1BA; 0171 834 5477 (bookselling)

British Horological Institute, Upton Hall, Upton, Newark, Nottinghamshire NG23 3TE; 01636 813795 (clocks and watches)

Gemmological Association and Gem Testing Laboratory of Great Britain, 27 Greville Street, London EC1N 8SU; 0171 404 3334 (jewellery)

Institute of European Business Suppliers, 6 Wimpole Street, London W1M 8AS; 0171 436 5468 (stationery and office equipment)

National Association of Goldsmiths, 78a Luke Street, London EC2A 4PY; 0171 613 4445 (jewellery)

Royal Pharmaceutical Society of Great Britain, 1 Lambeth High Street, London SE1 7JN; 0171 735 9141 (pharmacy)

Wine and Spirit Education Trust, Five Kings House, 1 Queen Street Place, London EC4R 1QS; 0171 236 3551 (wines and spirits)

11 Further reading

Three recommended booklets are:

'Careers in Retail – A guide to Retail Careers for Young
   People', available from the National Retail Training Council
   £2.95
'Your Career in Food Retailing and Wholesaling', available
   from the Institute of Grocery Distribution
'Retail Selling, Buying and Distribution', Association of
   Graduate Advisory Services Information Sub Committee,
   CSU Publications, £2.50. A graduate careers information
   booklet.

There are a number of useful and informative books on retailing
including the following:

*How to Buy and Run a Shop: A Practical Guide to Successful
   Retailing*, Iain Maitland, How To Books, 1995, £8.99
Off Our Trolleys: Food Retailing and the Hypermarket Economy,
   Tim Lang, Institute for Public Policy Research, 1995,
   £4.95
Law For Retailers, Bill Thomas, Management Books 2000, 1996,
   £12.99
Marketing, Retailing and Sales Casebook, Hobsons Casebooks,
   Hobsons Publishing, 1994, £7.99
Retail Selling, Peter Fleming, Management Books 2000, £12.99
Retailing: Principles and Practices, Dale M Lewison and M Wayne
   Delozier, Merrill, 1989, £3.50

Two highly recommended small books on how to get a job:

Finding a Job, Louise Bostock Lang, HarperCollins, 1996, £4.99
The Book of Career Questions: 200 questions which will change the whole of your working life, Max Eggert, £2.50

12 Useful addresses

British Retail Consortium, 5 Grafton Street, London W1X 3LB; 0171 647 1500

British Shops and Stores Association, Middleton House, 2 Main Road, Middleton Cheney, Banbury, Oxfordshire OX17 2TN; 01295 712277

Business and Technology Education Council (BTEC), c/o Edexcel Foundation, Stewart House, 32 Russell Square, London WC1B 5DN; 0171 393 4444

Central Application Office (Degrees), Tower House, Eglington Street, Galway, Republic of Ireland

City & Guilds of London Institute, 1 Giltspur Street, London EC1A 9DD; 0171 294 3167

Department of Employment (Head Office), Moorfoot, Sheffield S1 4PQ; 0114 276 8644

Department of Employment (London), Caxton House, Tothill Street, London SW1H 9NF; 0171 273 6969

Distributive OSC, The Coda Centre, 189 Munster Road, London SW6 6AW; 0171 386 5599

National Federation of Retail Newsagents, Yeoman House, 11 Sekforde Street, Clerkenwell Green, London EC1R 0HA

National Retail Training Council, 5 Grafton Street, London W1X 3LB; 0171 647 1500

Radio, Electrical and Television Retailers' Association Ltd, RETRA House, St John's Terrace, 1 Ampthill Street, Bedford MK42 9EY; 01234 269110

Retail Training Consultancy Council, 1 Glenville Terrace, Dublin 14, Republic of Ireland; 01 298 2722

Scottish Distributive Industries Training Council, The Beta Centre, University of Stirling Innovation Park, Stirling FK9 4NF; 01786 451661

Scottish Vocational Education Council, Assessment Services Unit, 24 Douglas Street, Glasgow G2 4NQ; 0141 248 7900

Union of Shop, Distributive and Allied Workers (USDAW), 188 Wilmslow Road, Manchester M14 6LJ; 0161 224 2804

Universities and Colleges Admissions Service (UCAS), P O Box 67, Cheltenham, Gloucestershire GL50 3SF; 01242 222444

Index

The Kogan Page *Careers in...* series

Careers in Architecture *(5th edition)*

Careers in Computing and Information
Technology *(new title)*

Careers in Journalism *(8th edition)*

Careers in the Police Service *(5th edition)*

Careers in Retailing *(6th edition)*

Careers in Teaching *(7th edition)*

Careers in Television and Radio *(7th edition)*

Careers in the Travel Industry *(6th edition)*

Careers Using English *(new title)*

Careers Working with Animals *(8th edition)*